MEET TOM BRADY

Football's Famous Quarterback

Ethan Edwards

PowerKiDS press.

New York

Published in 2009 by The Rosen Publishing Group, Inc.
29 East 21st Street, New York, NY 10010

First Edition

Editor: Amelie von Zumbusch
Book Design: Greg Tucker
Photo Researcher: Jessica Gerweck

Photo Credits: Cover, pp. 4, 7, 8, 10, 11, 13, 14, 16, 18, 21, 22, 23, 26, 29 © Getty Images; pp. 15, 19, 30 © AFP/Getty Images; p. 24 © WireImage; p. 27 © Associated Press.

Library of Congress Cataloging-in-Publication Data

Edwards, Ethan.
    Meet Tom Brady : football's famous quarterback / Ethan Edwards. — 1st ed.
        p. cm. — (All-star players)
    Includes index.
    ISBN 978-1-4042-4492-4 (library binding)
    1. Brady, Tom, 1977– —Juvenile literature. 2. Football players—United States—Biography—Juvenile literature. I. Title.
    GV939.B685E39 2009
    796.332092—dc22
    [B]
                                        2008007515

Manufactured in the United States of America

Contents

4

Meet Tom Brady

   Tom Brady is one of the most famous **athletes** in the world. Brady plays quarterback for the New England Patriots. The quarterback is one of the most important players on a football team. He is the leader of the team's **offense**. Some football **experts** think that Tom Brady is the best quarterback ever to play **professional** football.

   A good quarterback has to have a strong arm to throw the ball down the field. This is called passing. A good quarterback also has to be smart enough to understand **strategy**. Brady is an excellent passer and a great leader. He has helped the Patriots become a **dynasty**.

Tom Brady's passing skills help make him one of football's top quarterbacks. Brady has passed the ball for over 25,000 yards in his career as a professional football player.

Tom Brady was born in 1977 and grew up in San Mateo, California. Brady has three older sisters. The whole family was athletic, and Brady learned to play sports at an early age.

As a kid, Brady's favorite football team was the San Francisco 49ers. His favorite player was 49ers quarterback Joe Montana. In January 1982, Brady got to watch the 49ers play the Dallas Cowboys in the 1981 season's Conference Championship game, in San Francisco, California. The 49ers won the game, and Joe Montana completed one of the most famous passes in football history. Brady was only four years old, but he decided that he wanted to be a quarterback.

All-Star Facts

Brady is also an excellent golfer. He has played golf since he was only two years old.

Brady's hero Joe Montana, seen here, is widely believed to be one of the best quarterbacks in the history of football.

Playing for His School

Brady went to San Mateo's Junípero Serra High School. The school is known for its sports programs. Brady is not the only famous athlete to have gone to school there. Baseball star Barry Bonds and football star Lynn Swann both attended Junípero Serra.

Brady played football and baseball in high school. He was so good at baseball that major-league teams watched his high-school games. The Montreal Expos **drafted** him to play professional baseball right out of high school. However, Brady knew that he was better at football. He also knew that he wanted to go to college.

Although Tom Brady was a talented baseball player, he chose to play football instead of baseball in the long run.

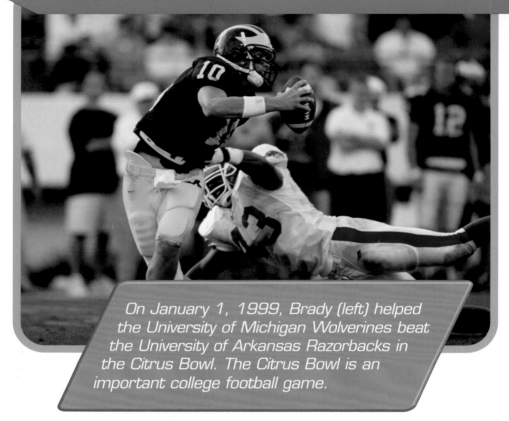

On January 1, 1999, Brady (left) helped the University of Michigan Wolverines beat the University of Arkansas Razorbacks in the Citrus Bowl. The Citrus Bowl is an important college football game.

Brady decided to play football at the University of Michigan. Michigan has one of the best college football programs in the United States. However, there were several talented quarterbacks already on Michigan's roster, or list of players. Brady had to be patient. He did not become the starting quarterback until his junior year.

Brady knew that he had to make the most out of this chance. Brady had an excellent season his junior year. He set three Michigan records in a game against Ohio State. Brady played even better during his final year. He was ready to enter the NFL, or National Football League, and become a professional football player.

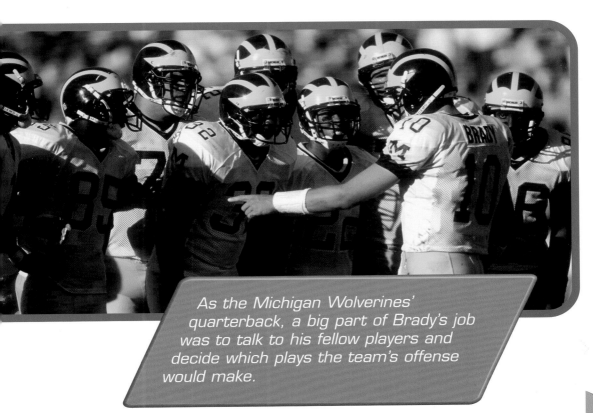

As the Michigan Wolverines' quarterback, a big part of Brady's job was to talk to his fellow players and decide which plays the team's offense would make.

Brady was good enough to play in the NFL, but nobody thought he would be a star. Most **scouts** believed he would be just a backup quarterback. Brady knew he could prove them wrong if he just got the chance.

The New England Patriots picked Brady in the 2000 NFL Draft. The Patriots already had a good quarterback named Drew Bledsoe. Brady knew he would have to be patient, as he had been at Michigan. Brady got his chance early in the 2001 season when Bledsoe was badly hurt.

All-Star Facts

Brady was the 199th player chosen in the 2000 NFL Draft. The NFL Network called him the biggest steal in NFL draft history.

In his first year playing for the Patriots, Brady got a chance to play in only one regular season game.

The St. Louis Rams were favored, or expected, to win the Super Bowl. However, Brady and the Patriots played much better than most people thought they would.

Brady made the most out of the opportunity. He led the **underdog** Patriots all the way to the Super Bowl. The Super Bowl is the most important game in the NFL season. The Patriots faced the St. Louis Rams. The Patriots played well, and the game was tied with only 2 minutes left. Brady had one last chance to lead the Patriots down the field.

The offense got the ball within scoring distance with only 7 seconds left on the clock. Then kicker Adam Vinatieri kicked a **field goal**, and the Patriots won the game! Brady was named the Super Bowl's Most Valuable Player, or MVP.

Brady and the Patriots were filled with joy after winning the Super Bowl in 2001. They beat the Rams 20–17.

Two More Super Bowls

The Patriots struggled in the 2002 season and did not make the **play-offs**. Some football fans and experts began to think that Brady was a **fluke**. In the 2003 season, he proved them wrong when the Patriots earned the chance to play the Carolina Panthers in the Super Bowl. It was another close game, and once again the Patriots won by only three points. Brady set a Super Bowl record by completing 32 passes.

Once again, Brady was **awarded** the Super Bowl MVP. He became the youngest quarterback to win the award twice! Brady also became one of just eight quarterbacks to win more than a single Super Bowl. Sports **journalists** began to compare Brady to his childhood hero Joe Montana.

Here, Brady hands off the ball to Antowain Smith (left) during the Super Bowl. Knowing when to hand off the ball is one of Brady's strengths.

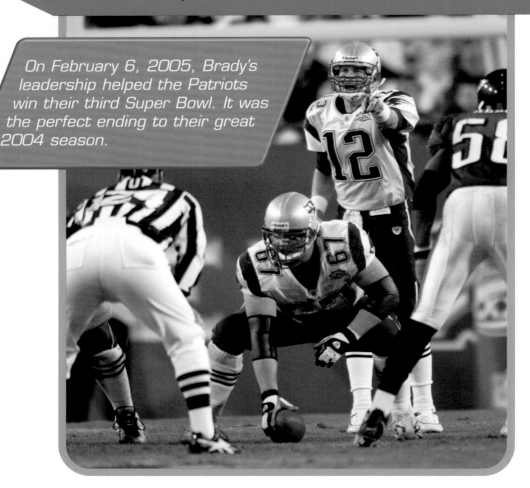

On February 6, 2005, Brady's leadership helped the Patriots win their third Super Bowl. It was the perfect ending to their great 2004 season.

The 2004 season was another great one for the Patriots. Brady led the team to their second Super Bowl in a row. This time, they faced the Philadelphia Eagles. Once again, it was a close game, and the Patriots won by just three points!

Brady now had three Super Bowl rings. Only two quarterbacks in NFL history had ever won more Super Bowls than Brady had. Brady was now one of the best quarterbacks ever to throw a football. He was also one of the most famous athletes in the United States.

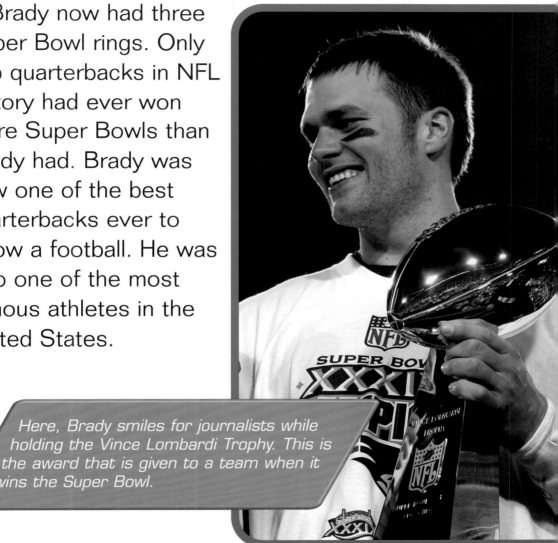

Here, Brady smiles for journalists while holding the Vince Lombardi Trophy. This is the award that is given to a team when it wins the Super Bowl.

The Patriots picked up some very skilled players before the 2007 season. One of them was Randy Moss. Moss is one of the most talented wide receivers in the NFL. Wide receivers catch long passes down the field. The Patriots were good before Moss joined the team. With Moss on the team, many people believed they were the best team in the NFL.

The 2007 Patriots went on to win all 16 of their regular-season games. No other team in NFL history had ever done this. Brady and Moss also became the best passing pair in NFL history. Brady's 50 touchdown passes became a new NFL record.

Tom Brady (left) and Randy Moss (right) played well together in the 2007 season. Moss thinks highly of Brady, and Brady has said Moss is "a very smart player."

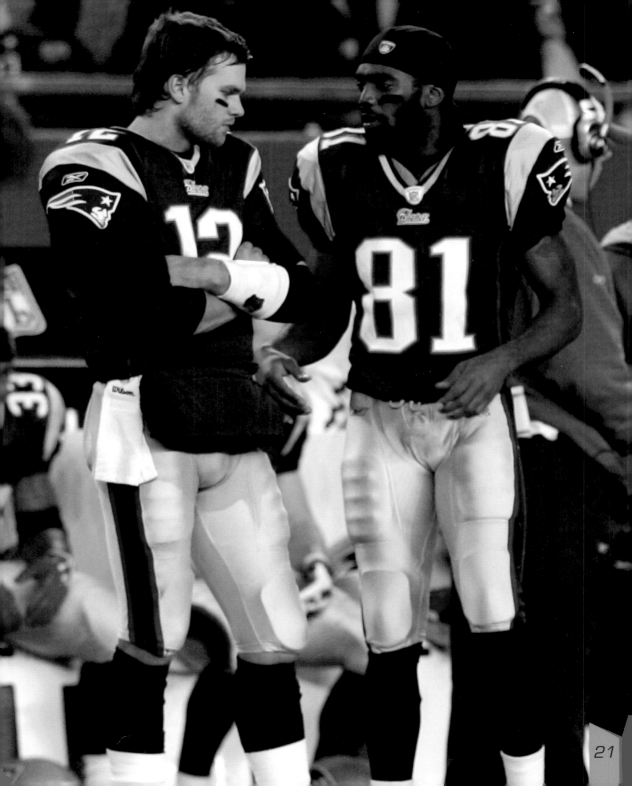

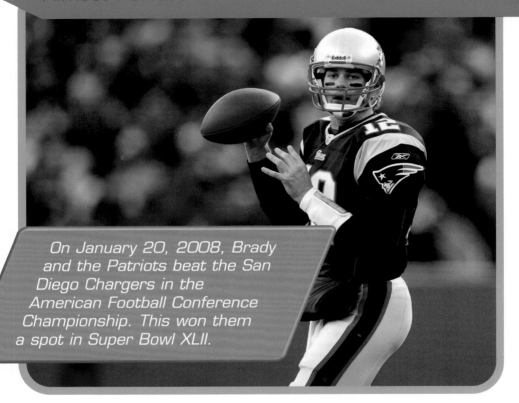

On January 20, 2008, Brady and the Patriots beat the San Diego Chargers in the American Football Conference Championship. This won them a spot in Super Bowl XLII.

Brady helped Moss set a record of 23 touchdown catches, too. The nation's top football journalists voted Brady the MVP of the entire NFL for the 2007 season. He received 49 of the 50 votes cast.

Brady led the Patriots into the play-offs. Experts agreed that the 2007 Patriots would be known as the best football team in history if they could just win the Super Bowl. The Patriots reached the big game. More people watched that Super Bowl than ever had before. Unfortunately, Brady and the Patriots lost a very close game to the New York Giants. The Patriots' final record for the season was 18-1. The only game they lost was the Super Bowl.

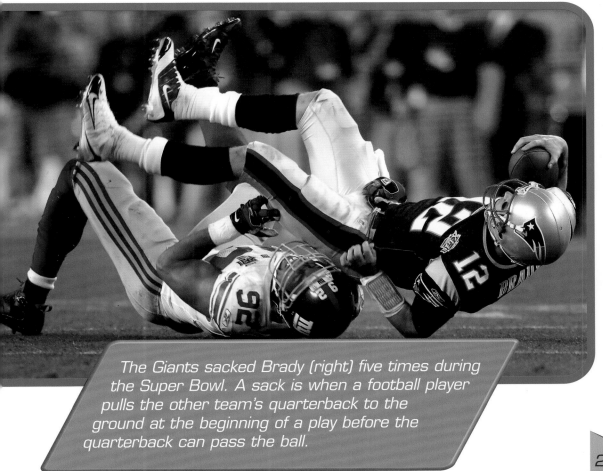

The Giants sacked Brady (right) five times during the Super Bowl. A sack is when a football player pulls the other team's quarterback to the ground at the beginning of a play before the quarterback can pass the ball.

Tom Brady is one of the most famous people in the United States. He was even a guest star on the television show The Simpsons.

Off the Field

Tom Brady is one the most famous people in the world. Even people who do not follow football know who he is. In 2002, *People* magazine voted Brady one of the world's 50 most beautiful people. He has appeared on the television show *Saturday Night Live* and had a small part in the movie *Stuck on You*. Brady is so famous that reporters follow him everywhere.

However, fame is not that important to Brady. He is committed to helping others. In the spring of 2007, Brady went on a tour of poor villages in Africa, with a group called DATA. DATA stands for debt, **AIDS**, trade, Africa. The rock star Bono and

All-Star Facts

Brady was one of the judges for the 2002 Miss USA pageant, or contest.

Millions of fans love and look up to Tom Brady. Brady has tried to use his fame to support good causes.

other leading activists created DATA to fight **poverty** and the illness AIDS in Africa. The goal of Brady's tour was to spread the word about the problems poor people face in Africa. Brady said that the trip showed him "the best and brightest of the human spirit." He learned that there are many things that people in America can do to help people in Africa.

Brady also works with his fellow Patriots to raise money for a **charity** called Active Force Foundation. Active Force Foundation designs sports **equipment** that can be used by people with disabilities.

Brady had taken part in many events to raise money for charity. Here, he is playing in the New England Patriots Charitable Foundation Annual Golf Tournament in 2005.

No one ever thought Brady would become football's greatest quarterback. He surprised the football world and broke records just by believing in himself. Brady is already headed for the Pro Football Hall of Fame. The Hall of Fame is a museum in Canton, Ohio, that has statues of the best players ever to put on a uniform. Many of the best players never make it there, but Brady almost certainly will.

However, Brady's playing days are far from over. There is no telling what other records he will break or how many Super Bowls he will win. There might never be a better quarterback than Tom Brady!

Some football experts argue that Tom Brady is on his way to becoming the best quarterback of all time.

Height: 6' 4" (1.9 m)
Weight: 225 pounds (102 kg)
Team: New England Patriots
Position: Quarterback
Uniform Number: 12
Date of Birth: August 3, 1977

2007 Season Stats

Passing Yards	Passing Completions	Passing Touchdowns	Quarterback Rating
4,806	398	50	117.2

Career Stats as of 2007 Season

Passing Yards	Passing Completions	Passing Touchdowns	Quarterback Rating
26,370	2,294	197	92.9

Glossary

AIDS (AYDZ) An illness that makes the body unable to keep itself safe from other illnesses.

athletes (ATH-leets) People who take part in sports.

awarded (uh-WORD-ed) Given.

charity (CHER-uh-tee) A group that gives help to the needy.

drafted (DRAFT-ed) Selected for a special purpose.

dynasty (DY-nas-tee) A powerful group that keeps its position for a long time.

equipment (uh-KWIP-mint) All the supplies needed to do an activity.

experts (EK-sperts) People who know a lot about a subject.

field goal (FEELD GOHL) When a football player kicks the ball between the other team's posts. This gets the team three points.

fluke (FLOOK) A lucky accident.

journalists (JER-nul-ists) People who gather and write news for newspapers or magazines.

offense (AH-fents) When a team tries to score points in a game.

play-offs (PLAY-ofs) Games played after the regular season ends to see who will play in the championship game.

poverty (PAH-ver-tee) The state of being poor.

professional (pruh-FESH-nul) Having to do with someone who is paid for what he or she does.

scouts (SKOWTS) People who help sports teams find new, young players.

strategy (STRA-tuh-jee) Planning and directing different plays in team sports.

underdog (UN-der-dog) Thought to be likely to lose.

Index

Web Sites

Due to the changing nature of Internet links, PowerKids Press has developed an online list of Web sites related to the subject of this book. This site is updated regularly. Please use this link to access the list:

www.powerkidslinks.com/asp/brady/